Say the sounds:
lick lick, huff huff,
waaah, flip flop, rustle

- What sounds do you
  think the family can
  hear?

- How do you think Dad
  is feeling?

1

Say the sounds: thwack, slip-slop, tchhhhh, clatter, chat chat

- What sound do you think the toy plane makes? What about the kite?

- What other games could you play on the beach?

Say the sounds: whoosh, pat pat, dip, dig dig, zoom, splash

- What sounds and smells are coming from the sea?
- What do you think Chip might find in his net?

Say the sounds: munch, crunch, flap, slurp, click, ark-ark

- Can you make the sound of the wind blowing?
- What do you think Biff is pointing at?

7

- Can you make the sound of Dad snoring?
- What sounds do you think you would hear at the funfair?

8